THREE SYLLABLES DESCRIBING ADDICTION

THREE SYLLABLES DESCRIBING ADDICTION

poems by

KATE DANIELS

BULL★CITY
PRESS

DURHAM, NORTH CAROLINA

Three Syllables Describing Addiction

Copyright © 2018 by Kate Daniels

Published in the United States of America

Library of Congress Cataloging-in-Publication Data

Daniels, Kate
Three Syllables Describing Addiction: poems / by Kate Daniels
p. cm.
ISBN-13: 978-1-949344-05-9

Book design by
Spock and Associates

Published by
BULL CITY PRESS
1217 Odyssey Drive
Durham, NC 27713

www.BullCityPress.com

CONTENTS

A Note to Readers

These poems are narrated by a character similar, but not identical, to myself, and represent other characters and situations that may be archetypal, emanating from many aspects of and perspectives on the current opioid epidemic.

Man takes drink.

•

Drink takes drink.

•

Drink takes man.

An old adage

We admitted we were powerless.

Step One

MOLECULES

Whether it's true or not, that all our
molecules replace themselves each seven
years, his body seems halfway new again,
one year into sobriety. I keep my distance now
but recall his painful, ten-pound freight, the torpor
of late term pregnancy. All those final weeks, I rested,
famished, calling for food I could spin into blood
and bones so he could thrive. Even then, his cravings
ruled us both. Mindlessly, he craved to grow,
taking what he needed from my willing body
as – two decades later – he would steal
what he needed from my dresser drawers –
bank book, string of pearls, his grandmother's
tiny chip of diamond-studded wedding ring.
The latter must have brought him almost nothing
at the *Cash for Gold* store where all the junkies hang out.

DRIVING

That was the year summer lingered
and fall came on late. I was still wearing
sleeveless clothes when the temperatures fell,
and the wind rose suddenly, and tore the leaves
from their branches in a matter of days.

By then, there was a long line of addicts
on the corner every morning – red-nosed
and shivering, sores all over, reminding me
of those roaming packs of starving dogs you see
in third-world countries. I shooed them away
when they begged for money... All that autumn,

I was searching for my son. Why I never looked
among the junkies on the corner who, after all,
were other people's sons, or why – *God help me* –
I drove right through their tattered clots,
and kept my coins to myself, and controlled
my thoughts – I have no clue. I just kept driving
though I had no sense of where I was going,
or what I'd do, or what I might find if I got there.

IN THE MIDST OF THE HEROIN EPIDEMIC

When I heard the news that Cynthia's daughter
had died, all alone, slumped over on the ground
beside a dumpster behind the convenience store
where she'd made her final buy, I logged off, and
walked outside to look at the water before I could think
too much. It's become a habit now – losing myself
in the soothing image of moving water before the headlines
and the stats start blaring out the way they do – performing
themselves inside my mind that has always imagined
too vividly too much... *You think too much*, my parents
always said. But thinking about this, or not thinking
won't reverse the events that have captured Cynthia
or bring back the daughter who's been carried away
in an opening chapter of a terrible plot. Addicts destroy
themselves – that's just where we start. And why
they might have wanted to, or if it was an accident
is beside the point... The aftermath is what's at stake.
The human flotsam captured in addiction's filthy wake.
Ordinary citizens like Cynthia with her stone face
and her dead blue eyes. Single mother of one child,
deceased. She works at the bakery down the block
from me. I pay her for a cappuccino and a buttered roll
every morning on my way to work. Afterwards,
I linger on the wooden pier, and drown my eyes
in the river's watery embrace, and lick butter
from my fingers, and fill my head with the strong smell
of hot coffee Cynthia poured for me. Small actions
that distract. They minimize, but can't efface,
any of the suffering.

BIRTH STORY: THE ADDICT'S MOTHER

She wasn't watching when they cut him
Out. C-section, you know. Green drape
Obscuring the mound of ripened belly
They extracted him from. He spilled
Out squalling, already starving. Still
Stitching her up, they fastened him
To her breast so he could feed. There
He rooted for the milk, so lustful
In his sucking that weeping roses
Grew from the edges of her nipples.
For weeks, they festered there,
Blooming bloody trails anew each
And every time he made a meal of her.
I know what you're thinking.
But he was her child.
She had to let him
Do that to her.

SUPPORT GROUP

For a long time, each day was a bad day.
Truthfully? For *years*, each day was a bad day.

The nights were worse, but she could slide
The deadbolt on the bedroom door, and swallow
An Ambien, or two, to summon sleep.

Thank god she never dreamed about it.

The meetings helped, but it was hard to go
Because the first thing you did was admit
You were *fucked* and had no power.

It was worse to stay home, sitting on the fear
Like a solitary hen hatching poisoned eggs.

There were a lot of rules and tissues in the room.
The rules were followed. The tissues were
Dispensed to those who wept.

Many wept.

In the rooms, there was infinite suffering.
It had 3 minutes each to describe itself.

A little timer went off, or someone waved
A cardboard clock face in the air. One Suffering
Stopped talking. Then the next Suffering started up.

A lot of suffering in the world, is the first clear thought
Most people have when they come here.

THE POWER OF NARRATIVE

Even with the sprawling, unbound stomach
of midlife, and the lumpy breasts she doesn't bother
to hitch up anymore, something makes her shine.

So in my mind, I call her *Gaslight Lamp*:
the kind you find on the townhouses
of the rich that flame steadily, non

stop, hooked up to some fossil fuel
source that energizes those generous pools
of light they shed, both day and night.

Like *that*, she walks around shining, lit
from inside but not by something shot
up, snorted, smoked. Years since that...

At a meeting once, I heard her tell her story
and had to step outside and take a moment
to clear those images from my head –

All that stuff about what she did to the kittens
and their mother cat... How would anyone *ever*
come back from that? But there

she was, and I could see her through
the window in her garish-colored
polyester slacks, her un-dyed

frizzy hair, and Walmart flats –
all her ordinary splendor –
the kind I never recognized until

I started coming to this room
with its cinderblock walls
and its stale smell of old coffee

where all I have to do is show up
and sit quietly and wait my turn
and listen to some stories.

THREE SYLLABLES DESCRIBING ADDICTION

Time breaks down, the therapist
Said in her practical voice, trying
To explain the nature of craving.

Time breaks down and stops
Going forward – it backs up,
Lurches and pools in long

Periods of stasis. Closed loops
Or broken circuits. *Yes*: addicts
Are fucked, and live out of

Sequence with everyone else.
While they're financing their next
Fix, robbing their own mothers,

Or screwing some stranger
Standing up in an alley, we're
Unraveling beside them, time-

Traveling ourselves all the way
Back to the start where it might
Be possible to blot all of us out

And put us out of our misery
Before this plot ever gets started
And pulls us into this future.

RELAPSE

Several of the young men
from the treatment center are
already dead. They spanned
the demographic spectrum
so no conclusions can be made
about why they did, or didn't, make it.
They just went back to using...

I remember their mothers
from the Family Program
where we gathered for a week
to educate ourselves about addiction
as "disease," and to learn
to not "enable," and
to practice letting go.

We held hands, and role played.
and chanted healing mantras,
and shared "experience, strength,
and hope." But in the restroom,
we dropped our masks and wailed
full blast, and held each other
and collapsed on the floor,
showing cell phone images
of our boys suited up for little league
and tumbling with their puppies.

Like every other addict's mother,
I have cried myself out, wrung
dry and ground down by the grief
and fear that fuels my weeping.
The single lesson I have learned
is this: A person can only feel
so much. Eventually, affect overflows
and loses shape as it escapes
from its container. If the thing
inside is hot? It scalds or scorches
Every part of us it touches.
And if it's cold, it freezes.

METAPHOR-LESS

The dryness dead center
Of deep pain. The bone on
Bone grinding that goes on
For months preceding
The surgery – that's the way
The parent whose child is using
Heroin again feels in the middle
Of the night unable to sleep, standing
At the bedroom window, looking out
Just barely conscious of what the moon
Looks like – drained, gray. The moon
Is a popular literary image – solipsistic
Misery, misplaced love. *Whatever.*
Tonight, it's nothing but a source
Of milky light, swinging high up in the sky
Shining weakly on the bleakness inside
And the bleakness outside that has
No other meaning but the cold
Un-crackable rock of itself.

100%

Is what she'll never be
Again. Not ever whole
Or complete. Never fit
Tidily back together
The way she was when she
First was. Broken now.
Forever, it feels. All
Her inner parts re-
Arranged in new patterns
She can't recognize.
And though human eyes
Cannot discern the lines
Where the paste pot
Pasted back together
All the broken scraps,
She can feel the shredded
Edges cutting her inside every-
Where the paper tore,
Sliding under the surface,
Striving for realignment
With where they were before
The needle loaded up,
And pricked through skin,
And found the vein, and
Plunged. Before the junk.
Before the junkie who once
Had been her daughter.
Or her son. Before all
That. Back when she was

Of a piece. When she
Was whole. Intact. Complete.
When she could still believe
Her child and she
Had once been
One.

PARENTAL

When the whole thing burst into flame
it burned outward from the center
and threatened the circumference.

The two of them were imprisoned inside.
They sat there helpless during the day,
and lay there crying every night.

Inside that ring, encircled by flame,
they prayed for the cleansing force
of conflagration they had read about

In the phoenix myth – how the suicidal
firebird strikes a match inside its nest,
and burns to death, but then comes back:

Its resurrected form ignited by one
unextinguished spark. That was the only thing
that kept them going – the argument they had

About the single spark: whether to blow
on it, or stamp it out.

৵   ৶

READING A BIOGRAPHY OF THOMAS JEFFERSON IN THE MONTHS OF MY SON'S RECOVERY

Because he bought the great swath of mucky swamp
And marshy wetland on the southern edge of the territory,
Then let it alone, so it could fulminate over time
Into its queer and patchwork, private self –

Because he forged a plowshare from paranoia
About the motivations of Napoleon, declined to incite
A war, and approved, instead, a purchase order –

Because he would have settled for New Orleans, but acquired
The whole thing anyway, through perseverance and hard
Bargaining, and not being too close with the government's money –

Because he bought it *all*.
               A half million acres.

                              Sight unseen –

Because he loved great silences, and alligators, and bustling ports,
And unfettered access to commerce, and international
Trade, and bowery, stone-paved courtyards, noisy
With clattering palms, and formal drawing rooms
Cooled with high ceilings and shuttered windows, furnished
In the lush, upholstered styles of Louis Quinze. Because he valued
Imported wines and dark, brewed coffees, and had a tongue
That understood those subtle differences, but still succumbed,
Thrilled as a child by the strange, uncatalogued creatures that crawled
And swam and winged themselves through the unknown Territory –

Because of all this, I return thanks to Thomas Jefferson
For his flawed example of human greatness, for the mind-boggling
Diversity of Louisiana – birthplace of my second son,
13th of December 1990, the largest child delivered
to the state that day...

*

Can't help drawing back at how he lived in two minds
Because he was *of two minds* like a person
With old time manic depression: the slaveholder
And the Democrat, the tranquil hilltop of Monticello
And the ringing cobblestones of Paris, France. The white
Wife and the black slave mistress...

*

Before he was my son, he was contained
Within a clutch of dangling eggs that waited,
All atremble, for his father's transforming glob
Of universal glue.

From the beginning – *before*
The beginning, before he had arranged
Himself into a fetal entity, and begun
Growing inside me – he was endangered
By the mind-breaking molecules our ancestors
Hoarded, and passed forward in a blameless
Game of chance, shuffling the genes.

Even then, two minds circulated inside him,
Tantalizing a brand-new victim with generations
Of charged-up narratives of drugs and drink,
Of suicide and mania, of melancholic unmodulated
Moods, bedeviling distant aunts who died early,
And wild cousins who loved their night drives
On dark roads with doused headlights, speedometer
Straining to the arc of its limit, mothers who danced
On the dining room table, kicking aside the Thanksgiving
Turkey, carefully basted hours before.

We marveled at him in his bassinette – such
An unsoothable infant, so unreconciled to breathing
Oxygen, wearing a diaper, waiting for milk.

Still small and manageable at first. But whirling
Moods, baby-sized, and effervescent
As the liminal clouds of early spring, stalked him
Even then. Even then
                    This Thing stalked him
Threatening his freedom
                    And his right to self-rule.

*

*We hold these truths to be self-evident, that all men
are created equal, that they are endowed by their
Creator with certain unalienable Rights, that among
these are Life, Liberty and the Pursuit of Happiness.*
                    from *The Declaration of Independence* (1776)

                    Before we *were*
Ourselves he knew us. Explained us
To ourselves. Gave us a language whereby
We understood the restless grandiosities of our forebears,
And set us off on our well-trod path of personal
Liberty and greedy freedom-seeking. Minted the metaphors
We go on living by, and misinterpreting, and clobbering
Over the heads of the rest of the world – Still,
His language stirs me up. Still, I believe
He was a great man, and seek, in the painful
Contradictions of his personal life and public
Service, ongoing signs for how to live
In *this* strange era.

*

*I know no safe depository of the ultimate powers
of society but the people themselves. And if we
think them not enlightened enough to exercise
their control with a wholesome discretion,
the remedy is not to take it from them,
but to inform their discretion by education...*
                                from *A letter to W.C. Jarvis* (1820)

Once more, we drive our son to the treatment center,
And sign him in, and watch him stripped of identity
And privacy. Shoelaces and cigarettes. Cell phone.
A dog-eared novel by Cormac McCarthy. A plastic bag
Stuffed with things we take away with us, and weep over,
Driving home. He has lost the safe depository of himself.
Is dispossessed. Is lacking any wholesome discretion
On his own behalf. Indicted by genetics, disempowered
By blood, how should we school him, except by love
And psychotropic medications?

*

Flight of ideas and verbal grandiosity:
Imaginary master of vast terrains, teeming
With fanciful creatures and wild weather:
A Louisiana Territory of a child's mind
Born there, after all, its doors and windows
Propped open to admit the gorgeous scenes
Of extreme weather, thriving in the rapid cycles
Of tropical heat, the *coloratura* of radical sunsets,
The tympanic symphonies of downpours
That dampened every day, and then were
Scorched dry by the blistering sun. Early
Symptoms we overlooked, and nurtured instead
As precocious tendencies of a burgeoning poet
Or a future president...

*

*The man must be a prodigy who can retain
his manners and morals undepraved by such
circumstances [as those of slavery].*

from *Notes on the State of Virginia* (1787)

In the long nights when I can't sleep,
When anxiety courses through my body,
Racheting up to a stiff rod of fear and dread
I feel impaled upon, I sometimes let my mind
Drift to Thomas Jefferson and his famous
Inconsistencies... Here he is, tranquilly
Trotting through the bracing sunlight
Of national history, all long bones and red hair,
The eloquent incitements of his discourse scrolling
Out the documents that determined our fate.
But there he is at night, other mind in ascendance,
Tying shut the bed curtains of a lover he inventoried
Among his personal property. With whom he made
Six children. Though legally he "owned" her.
And then "owned" them. His very own
Sons and daughters...

*

The way that two things can coexist without
Cancelling each other out – how did he live
Like that? *How does my own son live like that?*
As a schoolchild longs for certainty, I crave
An answer, and sometimes hold my two hands up
To weigh the *yes* against the *no*, slavery
In one hand, freedom in the other: a tiny exercise
In bipolarity that never helps.

*

Sometimes it helps to latch on
To someone else's vision
In a crisis – the way I did
At Monticello, so long ago,
Stumbling along the rain-slicked
Bricks of orderly paths. Working class girl
In cheap shoes and plastic glasses,
Bad teeth. Terrified by the new world
Of the mind I'd entered. From the strict
Arrangements and smoothed out edges
Of all those interwoven pavers someone baked
From clay, carted there, laid out by hand,
Brick by brick by brick, I carved a small sanity
Where I could rest. And read.

*

I cannot live without books, he wrote.
And so gave permission for a kind of life
Previously unimaginable: this life I live now –
Soothing myself and seeking comprehension
Among my many volumes.

OTHERNESS

What if the flowers in the vase
are suffering? What if they're not
the pleasure you thought they'd be
when you bought them, already cut,
lifted up from the florist's swirling vat
of spring's gorgeous offerings? Pink
tulips whose tubular green necks
stretch so gorgeously to the last
bit of sunlight they will ever gather…

        You bought them
as a joy to meet your eyes when you rose
from sleep. But what if your joy
is their undoing, their dying?
And if the petals dropped languidly
from the blossom's head are in some
other world a dismembering that moves
those alien citizens to what we might call
grief if only we could interpret
their different system of signs
and signals, if only we could feel
what they are feeling?

DRIED FLOWERS: VISION AT A HALFWAY HOUSE

When the full-flowering blossoms of early spring
Are at their prime, slice them from their stems
While they are still pliable and gorgeous. Before
They murder themselves with their own dark beauty.
Then bind them up in loose bunches, and carry them
Inside to the dry heat of a dark back room where
Televisions run all day, and cigarettes burn
Unheeded in ashtrays. Outside, the unchosen blooms
Have overtaken the garden. They will go on dying
Naturally, and in their time. But here inside,
The chosen few are stored away, instructed to rest
For as long as it will take to achieve the dried-out state
That mimics life and keeps them breathing. Humming
Their tuneless tune: *Not using. Not using. Not using.*

REGARDING THE BURNING OF BOOKS

Regret is the only book I've ever
Burned: I threw it into the fire

As a useless text, and resolved
To stand still for a while, and feel

The fire's heat, and not even try
To resist. The path backwards

Is overgrown anyway before we
Even reach its end. We already saw

Its sights and blistered our feet
And froze our asses off walking

There the first time. We know its
Start and stop. So why go back?

A bonfire built to burn regret
Destroys every pathway leading

Back, and wastes no energy lighting
Up the dark environs of the unknown

Future that lies beyond its flaming
Circle. Its message is fiery and

Stark: five syllables flaming
In the present tense: *It is what it is.*

A declaration, of sorts. A manifesto,
If you will. A way to live.

DETACHMENT

The things you love are still
Beautiful in the new dark
They live in now.

They're in their own stories
Part of a larger plot you're
Too small to see the sense of.

You can go on being unchanged
Yourself, still wrecking your hands
And throwing out your back, trying

To force open the window
That's been stuck for ages,
Or you can give it up, and sit

Still in the center of the room
And just breathe, and feel the grinding
Without trying to change it.

CREDITS & ACKNOWLEDGEMENTS

"Birth Story: The Addict's Mother," "Driving," "Metaphor-less," and "Support Group" in *Five Points*.

"Driving" was published in multiple formats by the Wick Poetry Center, Kent State University, including *Traveling Stanzas* (2018).

"Molecules" in *New Letters*. Nominated for a Pushcart Prize.

"In the Midst of the Heroin Epidemic," "Driving," "Molecules," "Relapse," and "Support Group" in *Vox Populi*.

"Reading a Biography of Thomas Jefferson in the Months of My Son's Recovery" in *p/m/s: poem/memoir/story* and in *The Mind of Monticello: Fifty Contemporary Poets on Thomas Jefferson* (University of Virginia Press, 2016). Nominated for a Pushcart Prize by *p/m/s: poem/memoir/story*.

❧   ❧

Grateful acknowledgement is made to Louisiana State University for permission to publish the following poems from my forthcoming full-length volume, *In the Months of My Son's Recovery* (Baton Rouge: Louisiana State University Press, 2019): "Molecules," "Driving," "In the Midst of the Heroin Epidemic," "Birth Story: The Addict's Mother," "Support Group," "The Power of Narrative," "Three Syllables Describing Addiction," "Relapse," "Metaphor-less," "Parental," "Reading a Biography of Thomas Jefferson in the Months of My Son's Recovery," "Otherness," "Dried Flowers: Vision at a Halfway House," "Regarding the Burning of Books," and "Detachment."

ON THE COVER

"Bird & Man II" (2002) by Robert Henry is used by permission of the artist.

ROBERT HENRY (b. 1933) lives in Wellfleet, Massachusetts. Born in Brooklyn, New York, he attended Brooklyn College where he studied painting with Ad Reinhardt and Kurt Seligman. He later studied with Mark Rothko and Hans Hoffman. Henry is Professor Emeritus of Art at Brooklyn College, and former president of the Provincetown Art Association and Museum. His work is available through the Berta Walker Gallery, Provincetown, Massachusetts.

ON THE AUTHOR

KATE DANIELS was born and raised in Richmond, Virginia. Educated at the University of Virginia, she later received her MFA from Columbia University. She is the author of four earlier books of poetry, including *A Walk in Victoria's Secret* and *Four Testimonies*. A forthcoming collection, *In the Months of My Son's Recovery*, includes most of the poems appearing in this chapbook. A former Guggenheim Fellow in Poetry, and a member of the Fellowship of Southern Writers, Daniels is professor of English at Vanderbilt University where she directs the creative writing program. She also teaches writing at the Baltimore Washington Center for Psychoanalysis and facilitates workshops on writing and recovery in Nashville and other communities.

RESOURCES

The worldwide fellowship of Al Anon provides support for people whose lives have been affected by other people's addiction and/or alcoholism. Al Anon is not affiliated with any church or religious denomination, political organization or party, and is completely independent of and uninvolved with treatment programs, hospitals, recovery facilities, etc. Al Anon's homepage is located at **https://www.al-anon.org** and offers information on the organization, and other ways to get help. Al Anon also maintains an active twitter account: @AlAnon_WSO

Al Anon groups are free, open to anyone who is bothered or affected by someone else's substance use or abuse, and anonymous. Lists of meetings are available online, as well as in local telephone directories. In most locations, meetings are typically available seven days a week, and are also available electronically and by telephone for those who live in far flung areas.

Al Anon groups do not recommend, review, discuss in meetings, or in any way endorse treatment centers, hospitals, halfway houses, etc. Al Anon's sole concern is with those who are affected by others' alcohol and drug problems. The contacts made with people in similar situations, however, may prove helpful or informative outside the formal structure of the group meetings.

For issues relating to dual diagnosis—co-occurring addiction and mental health issues—consult your physician and/or mental health experts. NAMI—the National Alliance on Mental Illness—sponsors NAMI Family Support Groups that operate similarly to Al Anon groups: community-based, free of charge, and confidential. Their homepage is located at:

https://www.nami.org/Find-Support/NAMI-Programs/ NAMI-Family-Support Group

The Twelve Steps

1. We admitted we were powerless over alcohol—that our lives had become unmanageable.

2. Came to believe that a Power greater than ourselves could restore us to sanity.

3. Made a decision to turn our will and our lives over to the care of God as we understood Him.

4. Made a searching and fearless moral inventory of ourselves.

5. Admitted to God, to ourselves, and to another human being the exact nature of our wrongs.

6. Were entirely ready to have God remove all these defects of character.

7. Humbly asked Him to remove our shortcomings.

8. Made a list of all persons we had harmed, and became willing to make amends to them all.

9. Made direct amends to such people wherever possible, except when to do so would injure them or others.

10. Continued to take personal inventory and when we were wrong promptly admitted it.

11. Sought through prayer and meditation to improve our conscious contact with God as we understood Him, praying only for knowledge of His will for us and the power to carry that out.

12. Having had a spiritual awakening as the result of these steps, we tried to carry this message to others, and to practice these principles in all our affairs.